"The amazing thing about the FOSTER™ Conversation method is how widely applicable it is to a high school student audience, experienced business professionals, and everyone in between. In just three days last week, I saw a high school student credit FOSTER™ for an award winning internship experience and then heard a broad group of our business community describe a FOSTER™ seminar as the best training experience they ever had. The FOSTER™ Seminar with a FOSTER™ book to reinforce the learning is a powerful combination that will help develop strong personal and professional relationships."

- John L. Chmarney
President, Lancaster (NY) Area Chamber of Commerce

To Order Additional Copies Of:

FOSTER™

Exceptional Conversation Skills
(For the Rest of Us)

Visit: **http://www.amazon.com**
or: **www.fosterconversation.com**

FOSTER ™

EXCEPTIONAL CONVERSATION SKILLS

(For the Rest of Us)

---

by RON RUGGIERO

Buffalo Printing Co., New York

This book contains the complete text of the
electronic edition found on the world wide web.

FOSTER™ – EXCEPTIONAL CONVERSATION SKILLS (FOR THE REST OF US)

Original Cover Design, Illustration and Artistic
Consultation by Susan Cabri Ruggiero

Current Cover and Printing by Buffalo Printing Company, Kenmore, NY
Photography by Accent Photography, Lancaster, NY

ISBN: 978-1-4675-9685-5

Printed in the United States of America

DISCLAIMER

Although the author has made every effort to ensure that the information in this book was correct at press time, the author does not assume and hereby disclaims any liability to any party for any loss, damage, or disruption caused by errors or omissions, whether such errors or omissions result from negligence, accident, or any other cause.

A special note of thanks goes to Patrick Kelley for his significant contribution to this project.

An additional thank you goes to Mark Kmidowski, Luke Otto, and, of course, my dear family and friends.

This book is dedicated to Doreen.

Thank you for sharing this fulfilling life of love and happiness with me.

FOSTER™

TABLE OF CONTENTS

PREFACE

FOSTER™ was created to provide a simple, easy to remember system for having a conversation with anyone. It was designed to be immediately accessible to anyone who reads the story. Over the years it has been proven effective with everyone from high school students to Fortune 500 salespeople.

I studied Mechanical Engineering at the State University of New York at Buffalo. Upon graduation in 1990, I was hired as an equipment designer. My employer was based in New York, and I worked in an office-setting based at the company headquarters. After one year, I was promoted to our sales engineering team. Within weeks, I discovered that effective communication skills were a critical part of the skill-set for a sales engineer.

While I always have been a person that was comfortable within my own circle of family and friends, I was not particularly comfortable engaging people who were newly introduced to me. Despite this fact, my employer had the bright idea that I should entertain customers when they came to our facility. Typically, our customers would spend a few days at the manufacturing facility testing the equipment they purchased. It was my responsibility to host our customers and to ensure that their experience at our facility was a positive reflection of the company. Generally speaking, our customers were not a particularly outgoing bunch, so I sensed a challenge in front of me. My days were spent giving tours of the facility and conversing about technical questions. I was able to connect on the business level, but I was struggling to make a connection beyond technical talk with our customers.

At the end of the day, I would spend the evenings with our customers visiting the area and sharing an evening meal. During this time, I would sometimes feel uncomfortable. I'd ask a few questions and exchange forced pleasantries in between minutes of awkward silence. The conversations felt forced and unnatural. I wanted to change this.

While I was working through this challenge, business was very good for our company. Sales increased and this provided me with the opportunity to improve my skills at building rapport with our customers. I read classic books like *HOW TO WIN FRIENDS AND INFLUENCE PEOPLE* and began to put some of the skills into practice. The ideas were great, but I found that I would often blank out on topics to talk about when meeting a new person.

That's when my little "friend", FOSTER™, changed my life.

Since then I have personally used FOSTER™ with hundreds of customers, seen it incorporated into high school curriculum, and trained a Fortune 500 sales force on its simple and useful method. I have also personally seen the transformation it can bring to individuals who were previously unable to truly connect with others. From business professionals to teenagers, FOSTER™ has been proven effective, easy to use, and immediately memorable.

I hope you'll find it worthwhile and effective for you.

Ron Ruggiero
Buffalo, New York

Create a Coincidence

*

ABOUT THE AUTHOR

Ron Ruggiero

Ron has been consistently recognized as a highly effective communicator and trainer within his profession. His career includes over twenty-five years as a global sales and marketing professional primarily in the healthcare industry. He has been invited to speak at industry forums throughout the world and has authored several articles for industry trade journals. Ron has also delighted in preparing and conducting original sales communication, negotiation, and presentation training sessions that have shaped the direction of professional sales teams on a global scale. For more information about the author, you may contact him through www.fosterconversation.com.

INTRODUCTION

"If it's your job to eat a frog, it's best to do it first thing in the morning. And if it's your job to eat two frogs, it's best to eat the biggest one first." - Mark Twain

Today we are awash in a flood of communication tools but we seem to have lost the ability to communicate. It wasn't always this way. The ancient Greeks considered the art of communication to be a critical element of a well-rounded education. The ability to hold a conversation was considered essential to professional or societal success from the Renaissance through the Victorian period. Today, our modern education system puts absolutely no training or emphasis on this subject. Surveys of corporations consistently report that an inability to get along with others is one of the most frequent reasons for employee termination. Business books clearly identify that the key skill to career advancement is effective communication. We know it is important, but we assume that "it just happens." Unfortunately, the ability to hold a conversation does not just happen. The American Academy of Child and Adolescent Psychiatry reports that American children watch an average of three to four hours of television a day. In generations past this time would have been spent conversing with friends and family. These trends have all contributed to many people having a hard time striking up and carrying a conversation with somebody new.

Many people have natural charisma and communication skills, and then there are the rest of us who weren't born as fortunate. The rest of us have read the books loaded with clever ideas and ways to sound witty and interesting. Unfortunately, the rest of us don't drink tea with an extended pinky, so this type of advice doesn't feel genuine. Are you one of those people who have a hard time meeting people? Do you view networking as a four-letter word? Is making small talk painful for you? Are you a salesman missing out on sales because you can't create rapport with your customers? Fear not. FOSTER™ will have you striking up and sustaining conversations within sixty minutes. The best part is that you will remember this system instantly and will be able to call upon it at any time. There is no study and you only need to read the story to grasp its elegant simplicity.

Do you dread going to parties where you don't know anyone? Do you feel like you'd like to make more connections and friends, but get tongue tied when you meet new people?

The goal with FOSTER™ is to be able to start and sustain a conversation with anyone. This conversation provides an opportunity for a relationship to blossom, a business connection to be made, or to simply pass the time in friendly conversation. Most people do not have a rational or logical system for conversing with somebody new. Too often conversations fail and the opportunity to connect with someone new is lost.

Struggling to connect with new people is stressful. Whether in work or our personal lives these uncomfortable interchanges can be a source of great stress and discomfort. This stress stems from two insecurities: what if they reject me and what if I don't have anything to say?

Do you have people in your life who make you feel like you are a million bucks? Think hard and you'll come to realize that they all show a deep interest in YOU. That's right, what makes them so fun to be around is that they are interested in what you have to say, think, and do.

The simple brilliance of the FOSTER™ model is that it makes the person you are trying to connect with feel like a million bucks. It does that by centering the conversation on them.

The classic by Dale Carnegie, *HOW TO WIN FRIENDS AND INFLUENCE PEOPLE*, tells us to "Be Genuine." This advice is perhaps the most important element when it comes to being a good conversationalist. You can't fake interest. Pretty soon the other party senses that your mind is elsewhere and they begin drifting away from the conversation. Being truly interested in what they say will enable you to identify common points and those will blossom into a conversation.

Put the other person first in the conversation. How many times have you had a conversation with a person whose only goal was to reinforce how important they are? It is a turnoff and as soon as the other party starts boasting you start looking for the door. Let the other person be the star of the show.

Insecurity about having enough to talk about with the other person is the other natural fear we have when striking up a conversation. FOSTER™ allows you to overcome that fear by giving you a set of tools or a framework to easily guide the conversation and allow the other person to talk about the subject they like best – themselves.

Catherine Blyth writes poignantly in her book, *THE ART OF CONVERSATION,* that: "great conversationalists listen more than talk. The main reason listening is overlooked is that its' masters deflect attention and cast it flatteringly elsewhere." Be a good active listener. God gave you two ears and one mouth for a reason. Use your ears more in the conversation than your mouth. Active listening isn't just about not speaking it's also about recognizing another person's comments and showing that you are paying attention. Nodding, showing attention, and prodding the other party to keep talking are just a few of the elements. There are many great books on the subject.

Now that we've reviewed these few practices it is time to come face to face with the real FOSTER™, a simple formula designed to help you do just that – start a conversation and keep it going for as long as you like.

FOSTER™ helps you to have this conversation. FOSTER™ allows you to relax. FOSTER™ allows you to make a connection each time you meet someone new. FOSTER™ gives you confidence.

The best part is that you'll be able to begin using FOSTER™ immediately and you'll remember it for the rest of your life.

*

You may only have

one chance

to create a deep and meaningful

connection

with a person that could

change your life.

THE CONVERSATION

I developed the following story from a variety of real-life experiences to help teach a powerful concept that I had created many years ago; a concept that has helped many people improve their conversation skills. My story begins like this…

It was early January and I had just finished a two-day business trip visiting customers in the North Carolina area. I boarded my plane for Cleveland, Ohio and actually looked forward to the one and a half hour plane ride to catch up on some work and relax a little. There was an open seat next to me and I spread my papers and notes out a bit. The plane's door was about to close and my empty seat seemed assured when a young boy of about eleven years old stepped onto the plane. On his back was an overstuffed backpack. A flight attendant led him down the gauntlet in my direction. I averted my gaze and tried my best to make the empty seat next to me invisible. The stewardess stopped at my aisle and pointed the little boy to seat 18B, my coveted empty seat.

I gathered up my items off the seat and arranged them underneath the seat in front of me. The little boy plopped down next to me, wriggled out of his backpack, and shoved its girth under the seat in front of him. In my mind, I could only imagine how shy he must feel sitting next to an older and bigger person. I looked his way and gave him the customary "airplane smile".

He met my gaze straight on, extended his hand, and said, "Hey mister, my name's Foster. What's yours?" Caught off-guard I couldn't help but give a little chuckle as I replied "Hello, Foster. My name's Ron and it's nice to meet you."

"Are you **FROM** Raleigh, Mr. Ron?" Foster asked.

"No." I replied. "I live in Buffalo. I was just in Raleigh for meetings with some of my customers."

"Do you live in Raleigh, Foster?" I asked.

"Nope, I was visiting my Grandma for the holidays. I live in Cleveland." he said.

Foster was silent for a few seconds and gave me the question that I've heard repeatedly for over forty years.

"Buffalo. Doesn't it snow a lot in Buffalo?"

I sighed and offered "Yes, it does snow quite a bit in Buffalo, but not nearly as much as most people think. In fact Syracuse and Rochester get more snow than Buffalo each year. "

Foster nodded. He was clearly impressed with my vast knowledge of upstate New York climate. I shifted the conversation away from Buffalo's fabled snow-lore and drifted it back to his part of the world, Cleveland. I let him know that my company's headquarters was located there and that I actually lived in Cleveland not too long ago. I then asked about how often he visited his Grandmother in Raleigh, and applauded him for being brave enough to travel alone. He said that this was the second New Year in a row that he had made the trip and was looking forward to going every year from now on.

Foster brought the conversation back to Buffalo, because he was curious if I was born there. Obviously my Cleveland comment created some confusion for him. I explained that I was born in Buffalo but had lived in Cleveland for a little while. I then added about how I actually had also lived in Raleigh for a short time many years ago. I helped him through the history of how my company moved me a couple of different times and explained that my daughter was born in Raleigh while my son was born in Cleveland. My wife and I had recently moved back to Buffalo to reunite with our families. It was important to us to have our kids raised alongside their cousins and grandparents. He said that he liked having most of his family there in Cleveland. He also explained that his visits to Raleigh to see his Grandma were so they could stay close as well. All in all it was a very nice little conversation.

Then, a short time later, as the beverage cart made its pilgrimage down the aisle, Foster looked at me and said,

"So Mr. Ron what is your **OCCUPATION** that it moves you around and has you traveling to Raleigh?"

I explained to him that I worked in sales for a company that makes hospitals and medicines safer. For the past couple of days I had been visiting some customers in Raleigh. I let him know that I actually travel around quite a bit and get to see cities throughout the world. The word hospital clearly struck a nerve. Foster shivered at the sound, and asked if I disliked hospitals as much as he did. He told me that he had his tonsils taken out at a hospital and it was miserable, except for the strawberry milkshakes.

"Foster, what would you like to be when you get older?," I asked.

"I think either a herpetologist or a history teacher, but my Mom keeps telling me that I should be a lawyer." Foster replied.

Foster said he loved both science and history, but his Mom was convinced that what he really loved was arguing with her. I laughed as a knowing parent would.

"Mr. Ron, what kind of a **SCHOOL** does a salesperson go to?"

I let him know that I graduated from the University at Buffalo.

"Did you get a sales degree from the University at Buffalo?" Foster questioned.

"No, I graduated as a mechanical engineer,"I replied.

"You graduated as a mechanical engineer? I thought you said you were a sales person?" said the perceptive little lad.

I replied "Yes, I do work in sales now. I took my engineering degree in a slightly different direction than most engineers."

Foster then asked why I went to college to become an engineer. I let him know that I had always liked math and was pretty good at it. My Dad was an engineer also so it was something that I was pretty familiar with. Foster replied back with an air of pride saying that the highest grade on his report card was usually in Math class.

Perhaps Foster was beginning to like the idea of becoming a lawyer because he asked what kind of a school you have to go to in order to become one. I let him know that you typically go to a college or university but then have to go a few more years after that to Law School. "So how many years of college is that?" Foster anxiously asked. I let him know it typically would be about seven years after he graduates from high school. Foster didn't seem completely overwhelmed, but the thought of it seemed to make him want to move on to something else.

I asked him what his favorite part of the school day was. "Gym!" was his reply. I chuckled. Foster quickly added that basketball and floor hockey were his two favorite units. He proudly let me know that he had scored a hat trick in floor hockey the last time they played just before the school break arrived.

I was about to enter into a tirade on the lack of a Stanley Cup from my Buffalo Sabres so far when Foster saved me with a question that took our conversation in a different direction.

He said "So it must be pretty cool to have to travel around with your job. What's your favorite place to **TRAVEL?**"

"Italy, hands down." I replied.

"Why Italy?," Foster asked curiously. I let him know that all of my Grandparents were born in Italy and moved to the United States back in the 1920's. I also let him know that Italy was not only a great place to go for work, but that I also loved our family vacation there.

I then asked Foster what was the best vacation that he had ever been on. He took some time before replying. He clearly had been on more than a few memorable ones in his short time. After an extended, pensive pause, he replied that his favorite vacation was actually a rather simple one. While his family had done the traditional Disney trips and beach resorts, his truly favorite vacation always involved his family being together and camping in a tent at a campground. At night, his Dad would point out the various constellations in the sky until he had them committed to memory. And together, they would have a race to see who could find the first satellite passing over them in the night sky. Clearly, this young boy is well on his way to becoming a very thoughtful and caring person.

Foster reached into his backpack and pulled out an apple that he had stowed away. The zest in which he ate it made me realize that he was hungry. I asked him if his apple was as tasty as he made it seem and he replied "Oh yes! I'm starving. But then again, I'm always starving!" Foster then asked me "So what's your favorite food to **EAT**, Mr. Ron?"

It was such a simple question but it opened up so many thoughts. I started thinking about the favorite food I like to cook, what I like to eat when I'm home, what I like to eat while I'm out, my favorite restaurant, his favorite restaurant, his favorite food...the options seemed unlimited. While I had that buzzing through my mind, I realized that I still needed to answer his question so I responded with "A nice pot of homemade spaghetti sauce and some fresh pasta. Both my Mom and my wife make a great pot of sauce." Foster gave me a big smile and asked "Does their sauce have a secret ingredient that makes it better?" I'll never tell. He said that spaghetti with a giant meatball or two was one of his favorite things to eat as well. He spoke how his family would go out about once a month or so to a great little Italian restaurant near his home. He laughed as he told me how fun it was to see his parents toasting their glass of wine with the owner of the place when he would stop by their table and begin to sing out loud. He also noted how "amazingly good" their cannoli is for dessert.

I think we were somewhere over Columbus, Ohio when Foster re-directed our conversation once again. He said "Mr. Ron, I told you about how I like to play basketball and hockey, what do you like to do for **RECREATION** when you're not working?" Now this really brought a smile to my face. I was so excited to tell Foster about how much I enjoy spending time with my kids and coaching my son's baseball team. I also let him know that, when I have some extra time, I like to play some golf or go to the movies with my wife. "What kinds of <u>movies</u> do you like to watch?," Foster asked. I replied that I like action movies and my wife likes romantic comedies. That meant that we exclusively saw romantic comedies. Foster laughed and told me about his parents and their famous "date nights". He loves their date nights because his babysitter will let him stay up extra late before bed and eat more snacks than would be allowed by his parents…truly a win-win for both of their sides.

Suddenly, in the middle of the next thing that I was about to say, the plane touched down. I had to look at my watch twice to believe that more than an hour had just passed. I collected my things and said my final goodbye to young Foster. He gave me a wave and a grin, grabbed his overstuffed backpack, and ran up the jetway to the waiting arms of his mother who was smiling from ear to ear. When I saw that lovely scene, I thought about Foster and the depth of the conversation that we just had. We talked about where we were from, my occupation, the schooling that we had completed, and the travels that we had been on. We spoke of the many foods that we love to eat and the recreational activities that we enjoy.

Where we were from, my occupation, our schooling, our travels, what we eat, and recreations.

From, Occupation, Schooling, Travel, Eat, Recreation.

FOSTER™

Foster, this young, unaware boy had just taught me how easy it is to have and enjoy a thoughtful and rewarding conversation with anyone, anywhere, at any time.

ENTER THE LIFE OF THOSE YOU MEET

I f you look back throughout the FOSTER™ story you will realize that there are words in bold capital letters. The first letter of each word form an acronym that spells the name of the imaginary little boy in the story. They also stand for the six topics of meaningful conversation: From, Occupation, School, Travel, Eat, and Recreation. These topics form the backbone of the FOSTER™ framework.

As you look back over the story you will also notice that some words are underlined. The second part of the FOSTER™ method consists of listening to the other person and continuing the conversation with follow-up questions. Each of those underlined words provided the basis of Foster's follow-up questions. In the conversation, he focused on one detail from the response, restated it, and formed a follow-up question around it.

The magic of the follow-up questioning lies in the simplicity of being a good, active listener. One of the essential elements of good listening skills is the ability to signal that you are engaged and paying attention to the conversation. By repeating a portion of what the person just said you are signaling to them that you care and that you are interested in what they have to say. Not only are you interested, but you would like to know more.

Critics of communication plans lament that such a program is manipulative. This program is not manipulative because it is designed to allow the shy person to do what comes naturally to so many others. It is no more manipulative than allowing the sight challenged to wear glasses.

Often we find ourselves in a situation where we feel stress *not* talking to someone new. We give a passing glance but never engage. Most people avoid a conversation with someone because they worry about not being memorable or interesting. Why would that person want to talk to 'boring old me?' Avoiding the conversation is the easy way out.

How many times do you see the same person over and over and "surface talk" without even remembering their name? This goes for everyone from the mom picking her kids up from school to the sales professional who meets clients weekly.

The FOSTER™ technique is designed to help you have the courage and provide the tools to dig a little deeper and enter the life of the person you meet. Watch any dinner table at most holiday gatherings and you'll see people talking for hours on end. This is comfortable because those people are already in our life. We trust them. We trust ourselves to talk to them. We know that we can talk about anything and probably do. It's the trust that leads us to that communication confidence.

But how can you gain trust quickly in a person that you have just met if the conversation stays only at the surface? You can't. Throughout the book, we will explore the connection that is tied to each of the topics. Where you are from, what you do for an occupation, where you went to school, where you like to travel to, the foods that you eat, and the recreational things that you enjoy. These subjects create the framework of a real conversation and a relationship.

FOSTER™ provides you with a path to explore and find mutual areas of interest in a conversation. In his book, *HOW TO START A CONVERSATION AND MAKE FRIENDS,* Don Gabor offers the following advice: "Changing topics is probably the easiest way to sustain a conversation while fishing for mutual areas of interest with your partner. You don't have to talk out one subject before proceeding to the next."

Warm-up Exercise

The simple act of talking to new people can be frightening. Making conversation a habit requires warming up and practice just like training your body. Give yourself time to get comfortable and used to this process. A study published in the *European Journal of Social Psychology* found that on average a habit required 66 days of practice before it became automatic. This exercise is a warm-up for your conversational skills.

For the next week, practice saying hello to new people and asking, "How are you today." I'm not advocating crossing the street to grab a stranger and saying hello. That would be just plain weird! What I mean is talking to the cashier at the grocery store, the person sitting next to you on the bus, the person in line behind you at the coffee shop. Use any potential social interaction as the chance to practice the essential skill of opening your mouth and talking to others.

FROM

"Home is not where you live, but where they understand you." - Christian Morgenstern

Most books on conversation tell the reader to avoid the question, "Where are you from?" FOSTER™ is a different approach. "Where are you from?" is a familiar, non-threatening question that opens up a conversation. There are tricks for sounding clever and making interesting small talk that shows how witty you are, but none of those things will do as good a job as asking, "Where are you from? The reason for this question in particle is simple – everyone is from somewhere. Asked confidently, openly, and with genuine interest, it becomes a great way to get a conversation started.

> *TIP: People who are from other countries or cultures can take offense to the "From" question because it can feel like they are being singled out as being "different" from the person asking. Consider using some of the variation questions at the end of the chapter instead.*

In many cultures throughout the world, where you are from defines everything about you. Intense bonding or hatred can be generated without knowing anything else about that person except where they are from. The reason is that they utilize the question solely as a means to find out if the other person is "on their team" or not. Our goal is not to judge the other person based upon their answer, but rather to suspend any notions whatsoever and just listen to find out more about them. In fact, your goal is to listen so the other person feels like they are the most interesting person on earth.

> **The Science**: Proxemics is the study of the impact of distance on interpersonal communication. An appropriate distance for introductory conversations in America is roughly four to eight feet from the person you are talking to. A distance of closer than this is generally reserved for communication with close friends. Many other cultures will consider half this distance appropriate for communication with new people.

Minimize your usage of shift-response phrases in your conversation and instead focus on support-response phrases. Shift-responses take the focus of the conversation away from the person talking and turn it on the other person. An example would be, "You are from Topeka, Kansas. I grew up in Nebraska. It was really nice……..". The shift-response takes the conversational initiative away from the person speaking.

Follow-up questions from the FOSTER™ model tactfully use support-response phrasing. Essentially these follow-up questions signal that you are listening and that you'd like the person speaking to continue talking. An example would be, "You are from Topeka, Kansas. Does it get very cold in the winter there?" You've allowed the person to continue talking, which is the goal of the FOSTER™ technique.

Your job is to begin and continue a meaningful conversation for as long as you choose. So you'll need additional follow-up questions. Here are a few potential examples based upon scenarios that we've encountered repeatedly.

VARIATIONS:

BUSINESS

How long have you worked here?

ROMANCE

What do you like best about living here?

PARTIES

"Where do you know the host from?"

WITH ACQUAINTANCES

"I don't think I know where you grew up, was it here?"

PUBLIC SETTINGS

"This is a great restaurant, are you from around here?"

Generally speaking the question, "where are you from?," generates an answer of a city. This factual answer is either the place where they currently reside or a different place. Natural follow-up questions should flow readily from either of these answers.

Depending upon the location and context of the conversation there are a million ways in which the conversation might lead. You don't need to steer the conversation down a particular path, just let it naturally occur.

Insightful answers that tell something of a fun experience or expose a playful view of the world are sometimes given when the question is asked. These may seem like a bomb waiting to go off, but it doesn't have to be this way. Give into the discussion and ask some follow up questions.

EXERCISE

Harvard researcher, Amy Cuddy, has discovered that adopting 'power poses' for two minutes can boost testosterone and reduce cortisol (stress hormone) levels. Before your next social interaction you are going to spend two minutes in private with your chin held high, shoulders back, standing tall with your hands on your hips.

We are now going to put the first chapter of FOSTER™ into effect. Our goal is to build true relationships so we are going to start off with someone we already know a little, but don't have a relationship with. Your goal is to approach them and say the following:

"Kevin, we've known each other for a while, but I don't know much about you. Where are you from?" Try to continue the conversation using variations of the follow-up questions presented. Don't prepare them ahead of time. Just take the conversation in the direction and as far as it naturally goes.

OCCUPATION

"Choose a job you love, and you will never have to work a day in your life."   - Confucius

Americans work more hours than any other country on Earth and largely believe that a job defines who a person is. Other cultures believe that a job is just one aspect of a person's life and that other parts are more important and interesting.

There are only 168 hours in a week and we spend almost one-quarter of that time engaged in our occupation.

> *TIP: Business bookshelves abound with advice on how to be a great networker. The simple key to being a good networker is to help others before helping yourself. Many times the occupation question provides you with an opportunity to connect your new acquaintance with another acquaintance of yours who may be able to help them. Never overlook the opportunity to do a good deed and help out the other person.*

Inquiring about occupation is a totally acceptable question, and it has its place in a conversation. In my opinion, that place isn't the first question asked. Asking it upfront makes the person asking sound self-serving and superficial. In a professional networking setting asking the person upfront "What do you do?"

is often the conversation ender because the receiver hears the question as "I'll quit having the conversation if your job is beneath mine or you are not useful to me in some way.

> *The Science*: *FOSTER™ is an extremely simple technique with some solid science backing it up. Research at the University of Grotinberg in the Netherlands has found that conversational flow increases feelings of satisfaction from a conversation and increases the belief that parties have similar opinions. Yet pauses in conversation, even short ones, trigger physiological responses of distress. Other research has also indicated that satisfaction in a conversation is directly related to conversational flow and is independent of the subject of the conversation.*

VARIATIONS:

BUSINESS

"Jennifer, in order for me to start the meeting with the right information would you mind if I ask what your role is here at your company?"

ROMANCE

"What do you do for work?"

PARTIES

"I'm really enjoying talking to you. What do you do for work?"

WITH ACQUAINTANCES

"We've known each other for a while, but I don't think I've ever asked what you do for work?"

PUBLIC SETTINGS

"Detroit is the home of General Motors. Do you work for GM?"

Retired people, the unemployed, and stay-at-home parents are a few of the people where this question may seem challenging. The answer, "I was laid off from work," could be very hard to respond to. Listening to their previous answers, having a real interest in the person, and using appropriate phrasing allows us to use the same framework.

"What line of work were you in before you retired?"

"What kinds of occupations are you interested in working in?"

"If you could do anything, what would it be?"

It is important again to keep the conversation rolling. Advice from the classic, *HOW TO WIN FRIENDS AND INFLUENCE PEOPLE*, is as relevant today as it was 100 years ago: "Have a sincere interest in your fellow man."

Follow-up questions:

What is your job like on a day to day basis?

Do you like being a (that occupation)?

How did you get into (that occupation)?

Is the job rewarding?

Do you like working for your employer?

EXERCISE

Pick someone that you know and have a conversation about their job. Start off the conversation by saying, "I'm curious about your career. Can you tell me what it's like to work as a (their occupation)? Try to ask three more follow-up questions centered on specific details that they have already provided.

"Life grants nothing to us mortals without hard work."

- Horace

*

SCHOOLING

"Education is what remains after one has forgotten what one has learned in school." - Albert Einstein

S
chooling is the third element of the FOSTER™ subject matter. Schooling is a safe question and a logical follow-up area for discussion after OCCUPATION. The goal in using FOSTER™ is to have a conversation with the other person, not to pass judgment or pigeonhole them into a category or personality simply based upon where they went to school or their level of education.

> *TIP: Active listening is a critical component of maintaining a satisfying conversation. Non-verbal communication like nodding and leaning towards the speaker are great, but often are just signals of being polite. True active listening involves hearing the person, processing what they are saying, and then responding in a thoughtful manner. Examples include restatement for clarification, paraphrasing, and asking follow-up questions.*

Roughly 40% of the US population aged 24-35 has a college degree; however college is not the only target of a FOSTER™ conversation. People tend to use level of schooling or school attended as another way to describe a person. He went to Harvard, Joan has a PhD, or Kevin went to Springfield High School can all be judgment statements about people. The goal by asking about schooling is not to define a person but to simply further our conversation and continue developing the connection. We've previously established where they are from and what they do for work, so asking about schooling is a simple follow-on question.

Follow-up Questions:

"Engineering is a tough field. Where did you go to school?"

"How did you learn to perform that job? Did your company provide training?"

"You are from Connecticut. I hear they have great public schools. Is that true?"

Any one of these questions about the subject of schooling can be appropriate and easily asked to prop up a flagging conversation.

> **THE SCIENCE:** *Personality types play a role in conversation. Recent research has demonstrated that shy individuals and outgoing individuals register the same brain response of wariness when presented with new faces. Familiar faces do not trigger this response in outgoing personalities. However, brains of shy personalities respond warily to familiar faces in the same way as new faces. FOSTER™ can aid shy people in gaining conversational confidence by eliminating awkward pauses and the worry of having to come up with new topics of conversation.*

Follow-up questions should be easy to craft as you are speaking with the person.

VARIATIONS:

BUSINESS

"Did you go to school for this role?"

ROMANCE

"You have an interesting occupation. Did you go to school for it?"

PARTIES

"Did you go to school around here?"

WITH ACQUAINTANCES

"Kevin, what high school did you go to?"

PUBLIC SETTINGS

"What kind of schooling did you need to get into that job?"

Many people interpret asking about schooling as snobbish, or only applicable to the college educated. This is simply not the case. Consider the following witnessed conversation:

Andy: "So Bob, you are a farrier. What kind of schooling do you go through to do that?"

Bob: "I apprenticed with an experienced farrier for almost 12 years before I started on my own."

Andy: "Wow that is a long time. How did you find out about horseshoeing as a profession?"

The conversation went on like this for 15 to 20 minutes. Neither party knew the other one, and Andy is a college educated CEO, while Bob never set foot in a college. The conversation was genuine, not coerced, and allowed the two of them to forge a connection.

EXERCISE

Use the subject of schooling to begin a conversation with someone whom you do business with. Begin sincerely with, "You do a really great job. Did you go to school for this?"

*

"A teacher affects eternity, they can never tell where their influence stops."

\- Henry Adams

TRAVEL

"Travel teaches toleration."   - Benjamin Disraeli

The desire to travel seems to be innate to human beings. Humans spread all across the globe driven by the desire to see over the next mountain and across the oceans. People put more effort into planning travel than almost any other activity in their daily lives. For instance, people typically spend several months planning a vacation, but only 15 minutes planning their retirement investments. Commonly experienced destinations provide a bountiful opportunity for deeper conversations.

> **TIP:** Conversational narcissism is a term coined by Charles Derber to describe a conversation where one person dominates the conversation without the give and take of a satisfying conversation. Avoid engaging in this behavior by limiting your use of shift-responses and focus on support-responses.

Follow-up Questions:

"Where do you travel for work?"

"Does that involve a lot of travel?"

"Where do you take the kids on vacation?"

"Where did you go on your honeymoon?"

"If you could travel to one place in the world, where would it be?"

All these questions are crafted around the concept of travel, and would take the conversation in wildly different directions. The common part of these questions though is that they are framed around the other person. Questions like, "We went to India last year. Have you ever been there?" can be a conversation ender because they can rub the other person's nose in their lack of travel. Don't use your conversation as a way to boost your own ego or standing. Use the conversation to boost the other person's ego.

> *The Science: Effective two-way communication between doctors and patients has been shown to positively affect symptom resolution, pain control, and emotional health.*

How would you use the travel question with someone who has never traveled? That can be tricky, but clues often arise in the earlier parts of your conversation that can guide you to the correct path. One example is the person who responds to a question on travel by saying, "I've never left the state, and don't want to." The follow-up question is very easy, "You must really love your state. What is your favorite part about living here?"

VARIATIONS:

BUSINESS

"Do you travel much for your job?"

ROMANCE

"If you could travel anywhere in the world, where would it be?"

PARTIES

"Where is the best place you've ever traveled?"

WITH ACQUAINTANCES

"I'm thinking of planning a vacation. Is there any place you'd recommend?"

PUBLIC SETTINGS

"Are you vacationing here?"

EXERCISE

Plan a hypothetical vacation based upon the information you gather in your next FOSTER™ conversation. Strike up a conversation and proceed to discuss travel. Base your "T" follow-up questions on your interest to potentially travel to that location for your next vacation.

EAT

"The trouble with eating Italian food is that five or six days later you're hungry again." - George Miller

Eating may seem like a trivial activity, but consider the role that eating plays in many cultures around the world. In Mediterranean countries it is considered absolutely mandatory to break bread with somebody in order to show hospitality. Food is lavishly heaped upon your plate, wine is copiously consumed, and the meal can stretch on for hours. Those of us with Italian grandmothers know all about this. "I'm so glad you visited me. Sit, let me feed you."

Other cultures share food from a communal bowl and eat with their hands. This tradition lends an intimacy to the meal. Theodore Zeldin writes in his book, *CONVERSATION: HOW TALK CAN CHANGE OUR LIVES*, that "In Jamaica, they have a system by which the locals invite foreign tourists for a meal, just for the pleasure of meeting strangers."

> *TIP: Dates often occur over a meal. Conversation within the date is often a main focus of stress, but often overlooked is how you treat the waiter. How you treat the waiter speaks volumes to the person you are trying to impress. Even though you are nervous, treat them kindly and honestly and you will be communicating that you are a good person to date.*

In America one only has to turn on the television and watch all the various cooking shows to realize that we love to eat as well. Eating of foods and remembering meals eaten evokes a strong sense of feeling. Foods are emotional. At this point in our conversation model you've covered many factual items about the other person, but now you are transitioning away from 'safe' background questions and into questions with more intimacy. This is a subtle change, but the conversation is moving towards an evolving relationship.

"You've traveled to China. What did you eat while you were there?"

"Pittsburgh is known for its food. What is your favorite thing to eat?"

"What is the worst thing you've ever eaten while traveling?

"Do you have a favorite thing to eat when you are at home?"

If you've been listening carefully to the conversation then you should have all kinds of ways to personalize questions about this subject. Children, spouses, hobbies, places traveled, places of birth, parents, tv shows, and lunches at work can all be ways of stringing together previous facts and this question.

One good suggestion is to avoid any comments on a person's looks when it comes to food. You don't want to assume that a person is thin and has a good diet only to find out that they have an illness.

> **THE SCIENCE**: Stress triggers a hunger-inducing hormone, ghrelin, but researchers at The University of Texas Southwestern Medical School have found that the hormone may also have implications for social behavior. The researchers engineered mice to be non-responsive to ghrelin and then triggered stress by using bully mice. The engineered mice exhibited more social avoidance and depression-like symptoms. The researchers theorize that the hunger hormone may have made our early ancestors less anxious in approaching new groups for food.

Inquisitive people collect facts like other people collect material items. They will read or hear a fact and mentally clip it out and file it into their brains for later use. Frequently in conversations something will be said that will stimulate these facts to surface. For instance, a person might say, "The climate in Tuscany was so wonderful." At which point the conversationalist may say something like, "I've heard that the climate is the reason that olives grow so well in Italy. Did you try any local olive oil while you were there?"

> **TIP**: When dining with someone for the first time and engaging in a FOSTERᴛᴍ conversation, be sure to order foods that are easy to manage and quick to chew and swallow to avoid awkward delays in response that could grind a conversation to a halt. Long strands of saucy pasta may be a fun dish to eat with your Grandma at home, but not with a prospective employer at a restaurant.

It is ok to use these facts, but try to avoid coming across as knowing everything about everything. It is a good habit to be humble and say, "I heard that Italy has the best olives. Do you know if that is true?" You have then turned your knowledge into a question that allows your partner in conversation to play the part of the expert. This is flattering to anyone and shows the conversationalist to be a gracious partner.

VARIATIONS:

BUSINESS

"We should sit down and talk over a meal sometime. Is there a food that you like best?"

ROMANCE

"What is the best meal you've ever eaten?"

PARTIES

"What is the craziest food you've ever eaten?"

WITH ACQUAINTANCES

"What do you normally eat for dinner?"

PUBLIC SETTINGS

"Is there a restaurant you recommend?"

EXERCISE

At your next mealtime explore the concept of food with your family or friends. Practice the "E" questions, by going around the table discussing favorite meals and foods that you could not live without. Try to ask three follow-up questions to each person at the table.

Enjoy each meal as if it is a truly special moment in time.

RECREATION

"Leave all the afternoon for exercise and recreation, which are as necessary as reading. I will rather say more necessary because health is worth more than learning." - Thomas Jefferson

John C. Maxwell writes in his book, *EVERYONE COMMUNICATES, FEW CONNECT: WHAT THE MOST EFFECTIVE PEOPLE DO DIFFERENTLY*, that if he had to pick a first rule of communication it would be to look for common ground. The final segment of our conversational model is probably the one most likely to uncover common ground and similar passions. Recreation, hobbies, and passions are the spice of a person's life. Asking questions about these subjects provides the person with the chance to talk endlessly about the things that they love most in the world.

> *TIP: Conversation skills are often derided as being phony and manipulative. There is no secret to being perceived as genuine. The answer is to truly be genuine with your intentions and be fully present in the conversation.*

Be aware that this question can open the proverbial Pandora's box, because the other person may never stop talking about their love of ancient Celtic warfare or yellow-banded parakeets.

Examples:

"What do you like to do for fun when you aren't ....?"

"Do you have any hobbies in New York?"

"What kinds of activities do you enjoy doing with your family?"

"If you could spend all your time doing one thing, what would that be?"

It is at this point in the conversation that you may very well discover a common love of rock climbing, modern poetry, or monster truck rallies. This can be the beginning of a beautiful lifelong friendship.

Story: My friend had a business meeting the other day with a customer whom he had never met previously. They talked throughout their business meeting, but while the conversation was friendly it wasn't overly warm. They then went to lunch together and he began to use FOSTER™ to work on their conversation. The first five letters of the model carried the conversation until their food came. However, the conversation got to a whole new level when they began talking about RECREATION. The customer owned a small farm in Arkansas and owned several head of cattle. He talked for almost 30 minutes about ranching, feeding the cattle, clearing his property and all phases of farming. It was a really interesting conversation for my friend, because he had an interest in growing vegetables and raising chickens. The common bond aided their conversation and turned a business relationship into a true connection.

Finding out what people do of their own volition in their free time is like opening a window onto their soul. If your seatmate on the plane tells you that he writes self-help books in his spare time, you can probably talk for the rest of the day about why he does this, how he markets his products, and all the people that he has met as the result of his hobby.

The Science: Many people believe that participating in activities is simply child's play or an avoidance of work. Some interesting studies have recently shown light on why recreation is important in a productive, financially secure, and healthy life. A research study in Australia recently found that health correlates to participation in organized community activities. The study also found that low levels of participation correlated with low incomes. A study of US adults found that only about one-fourth of all US adults performed any activity on a given day and that only 61% had any activity at all within a 30 day period.

Follow-up Questions:

How did you get into your hobby?

How do you find the time to do.......?

VARIATIONS:

BUSINESS

"What do you like to outside of work?"

ROMANCE

"How do you like to spend your free time?"

PARTIES

"Are you involved in any activities?"

WITH ACQUAINTANCES

"What do you do with your spare time?"

PUBLIC SETTINGS

"What are the best activities to do around here?"

EXERCISE

We've moved through the FOSTER™ system and you are now ready to put the model into full effect. Share the program with your partner or friend. Make a challenge to each other to talk to the most people at your next social event using FOSTER™. Try to work through every letter in the program.

The FOSTER™ Profile: Now that you are able to start and sustain a meaningful conversation and make an immediate positive impact on those that you meet, be prepared to take the next step when you see that person again, at a later time. Create a FOSTER™ Profile by maintaining mental or actual notes on their F, O, S, T, E, and R stressing the key touch points of your earlier conversations. Asking a person how their vacation was or how their child did on that big piano audition, as you had discussed during your earlier conversation, will make them truly feel like a million bucks simply because you cared and made the effort to remember something that was very important to them. It will truly set you apart from everyone else.

Dance each dance,
and sing each song
for your own joy;
as if no one was watching.
- Anonymous

*

CONCLUSION

FOSTER™ is an easy to use system of conversation aimed at making you more confident and capable in conversation. As your confidence develops you will be able to branch away from the framework presented her, explore other topics, and adapt it to your personal style. Conversations will become easier, relationships will multiply, and you'll find that your life will open up in ways you never expected. The best part is that your little friend FOSTER™ will always be right by your side to rescue you when you struggle in conversation.

A journey of a thousand miles begins with one step. FOSTER™ only works if you use it. Learn to open your mouth and say hello to people. Make a game of using the program. See how many letters you can get through. It will feel artificial and contrived at first. Don't worry about that. Keep the conversation going by utilizing the letters. F is for FROM. Ask where the person is from. Frame a follow-up question about that location. Take the subject in its natural trajectory. Be truly interested in the person and what they have to say.

When the conversation wanes you can ask about what they do for an OCCUPATION. Use a follow up question based upon what they say. A good one is to ask about how they got into that line of work. People love to talk about what they do for work and this conversation can go on for quite a while.

When the subject starts to slow down you can transition into where they went to SCHOOL. Based upon that answer you can take the conversation in any number of ways. One way is to explore what it was like to go to school there. Weather, sports, education can all be potential areas for exploration.

The next transition point is to talk about TRAVEL. You can ask about vacation, work travel, best places ever traveled, or utilize any other information gleaned from the previous string of conversation. Travel is the beginning of a more personal conversation. You've moved from safe questions into questions that are more intimate. A friendly conversation will begin to include information about family and friends. Without work or effort you are now having a meaningful conversation!

When the travel portion of the conversation begins to slow down you can make the move to talking about what they EAT. It may seem odd to ask about what a person EATS, but the travel portion of your conversation has provided you with the perfect segue into a discussion of food. Travel is about experiencing different cultures and cuisines and people take the time during travel to savor food and enjoy tastes and flavors that they normally won't. They will talk all day long about these flavors, meals they enjoyed, and the best parts of their experiences. Follow up questions will be simple, obvious, and will last for a long-time.

You may never get to another letter, but if you do....ask about what they do for RECREATION. Work is often about necessity, but recreation is about choice and love. People will talk endlessly about their hobbies. You need to stay present, ask questions, and guide the conversation in a natural way.

Your next friend, lover, or business connection may just come from using your new friend, FOSTER™. Whenever you struggle with the conversation just think of Foster, picture his smiling little face while carrying that overstuffed backpack and run through each of the letters. F – From, O – Occupation, S – School, T-Travel, E-Eat, and R-Recreation. Your next, new conversation may just be with someone that turns out to be the most important person in your life.

The End.

SUGGESTED READING

"Amy Cuddy: Your Body Language Shapes Who You Are." *TED: Ideas worth Spreading.* N.p., n.d. Web. 09 June 2013.

"The Art of Selling; Schumpeter." *The Economist (US)* 22 Oct. 2011: n. pag. Print.

Blyth, Catherine. *The Art of Conversation: A Guided Tour of a Neglected Pleasure.* New York, NY: Gotham, 2009. Print.

Carnegie, Dale. *How to Win Friends and Influence People.* New York: Simon and Schuster, 1981. Print.

"Children And Watching TV | American Academy of Child & Adolescent Psychiatry." *Children And Watching TV | American Academy of Child & Adolescent Psychiatry.* N.p., n.d. Web. 09 June 2013.

Derber, Charles. *The Pursuit of Attention: Power and Ego in Everyday Life.* Oxford: Oxford UP, 2000. Print.

Gabor, Don. *How to Start a Conversation and Make Friends.* New York: Simon & Schuster, 2011. Print.

Lally, Phillippa, Cornelia H. M. Van Jaarsveld, Henry W. W. Potts, and Jane Wardle. "How Are Habits Formed: Modelling Habit Formation in the Real World." *European Journal of Social Psychology* (2009): N/a. Print.

Maxwell, John C. *Everyone Communicates, Few Connect: What the Most Effective People Do Differently.* Nashville, TN: Thomas Nelson, 2010. Print.

Schumpeter. "The Death of the Salesman Has Been Greatly Exaggerated." *The Economist* 12 Oct. 2011: n. pag. Print.

Stewart, Moira A., PhD. "Effective Physician-Patient Communication and Health Outcomes - A Review." *Canadian Medical Association Journal* 152.9 (1995): n. pag. Print.

Zeldin, Theodore. *Conversation: [how Talk Can Change Our Lives].* Mahwah, NJ: HiddenSpring, 2000. Print.